Getting the Most Out of your CRM

25 Tips to Increase Adoption, Maximize Value, and Increase Profits from your Customer Relationship Management System

by

WW Chee

I0477942

Books by
WW Chee

The Sales Operations Handbook

Getting the Most Out of your CRM

Sales Operations for Small Businesses

Managing the Sales Pipeline

Table of Contents

Legal Notes

Copyright 2017 - All rights reserved

This document contains opinions and ideas of the author. It is sold for the purpose of providing helpful and reliable information; the publisher, author, and all other parties involved in the making of this document are not required to render any qualified services or advice.

The information provided herein is strictly for educational purposes; any liability, in terms of inattention or otherwise, by any usage or abuse of any policies, processes, or directions contained within, is the solitary and utter responsibility of the reader.

Under no circumstances will any legal responsibility or blame be held against the publisher, author, or any other parties involved in the making of this document for any reparation, damages, or monetary loss due to the information herein, either directly or indirectly.

Permission is not granted to reproduce, duplicate, or transmit any part of this document in electronic or printed format. Recording of this publication is also prohibited and storage of this document is not allowed without the written permission from the publisher. All rights are reserved.

Introduction

The concept of Customer Relationship Management (CRM) was first mentioned in 1990's, with Sibel, PeopleSoft, SAP, and Oracle being the first generation of CRM software to evolve from sales force automation, contract management programs, and enterprise resource planning.

While this may make it seem like CRM is a type of software or technology, it has since become a lot more than that as CRM has evolved into a philosophy of putting customers first. All the systems, processes, functions, reports, and all other things associated with a CRM system is about facilitating that relationship between the organization and the customer. It is easy to forget that the focus of CRM is on the customer, but CRM does not need to be a complicated affair. Ultimately the purpose of a CRM system is that it allows organizations to be more effective in gathering data, interpreting it, and acting on it.

The philosophy of CRM is about building customer loyalty, and maintaining a relationship between your organization and the customer regardless of who is interacting with the customer. The system is what allows collaboration between departments, or even within the same department, ensuring that the customer's preferences, purchase history, and discussion points are noted and addressed.

The goal of implementing a CRM system is to have a more complete understanding of the customer, across all departments and levels of an organization. This will allow anyone who interacts with the customer to provide the same level of service and be on the same page when dealing with the customer. This improves the quality of the interaction, and the satisfaction of the customer.

While CRM systems are used by many departments and I try to adopt a universal approach, I have broken down my experience for getting the most out of a CRM system into 25 easy to follow points. These points are organised around 4 main categories:

(i) Implementation
(ii) Managing the System
(iii) Making Use of Data, and
(iv) Taking it Further

Implementation

1. Get the People You Need Onboard

When embarking on an implementation project, it is important to get stakeholder representation from all the business functions and departments that will be using the CRM system. Having input from various departments ensures that each department's use cases, concerns, needs, and wants are all addressed during the early phases. Otherwise the CRM system will not be fully utilized for its intended purpose.

The main people who should be involved in the project team are:

(i)   Top Management
(ii) Project Managers
(iii) Super Users (Champions)

Top Management

Top management drives the culture of the organization, their support and adoption of the CRM system is crucial to inspire credibility. Management's early adoption gives a synergy effect on the whole organization, encouraging the adoption from the rest of the organization as well. This is important because lack of adoption is one of the most common reasons CRM implementation projects fail.

The support of an executive sponsor will help drive the vision for CRM and articulate the business needs even if they may not be involved in the implementation. Top management has to use the CRM system and understand it; this gives visibility to the CRM system, the project team, and the super users.

When salespeople know that top management use the CRM system adoption rates will increase. Having meaningful conversations between the organization's top management and the sales department is crucial to showing support. This will help to get the organization on board with the CRM system.

Forrester Research, an American market research company specializing in the impact of technology found that not having a sponsor in a top management role greatly increases the risk of failure when implementing a CRM system. Therefore having an executive sponsor is crucial in driving adoption!

Project Manager

Aside from the executive sponsor, another key person when implementing a CRM system is the project manager.

The project manager has the mandate from management to drive the project and get things done. His or her role is to lead the change management process, and this requires someone who is able to collaborate well with other departments, with an intricate understanding of the sales process the organization uses, and the ability to pull off the project within the timeline and budget allocated.

Very often, a sales manager or someone from sales operations will fill this role. It is also possible to have a team of project managers with representation from each department using the CRM system, or have representation of some sort in the project team at least as subject matter experts.

Super User

A super user is usually a person or a group of people who are selected to champion the CRM system. Ideally a super-user will have both technical knowledge, and business (sales) process knowledge.

The super-user will be highly involved in the planning and implementation of the CRM, and eventually he or she will be a resource for support when users need information or have problems with the CRM. This person or persons is often also the contact point for the CRM software vendor, and will be the first to get information about new versions, updates, or news.

If the organization does not span more than one location, a super user would be sufficient, but larger organizations it is common to have a super-user from each region or office, to give more exposure and activity around the CRM and its associated processes.

Note that all administrators are usually also super users, but not all super users may be administrators; sometimes managers, analysts, and other users are given super user status for reasons of access, testing, or other functionality.

2. Have Clear Deliverables for the Project

As CRM systems requires significant investments in terms of time and money, therefore management would want to see returns in those investments.

Clear deliverables will make it easier to forecast the timeline, the budget, and the scope of the project. To agree on the deliverables, we should start by defining the objectives and the results that would be necessary to achieve those objectives. Example, if the objective is to deliver better leads to the sales department, the results that will drive that would be having marketing campaigns that are better qualified.

The deliverables for the first 30 days especially are crucial to management, as it shows the effectiveness of the investment in the project. This motivates the team members to continue driving adoption and getting the organization to use the system.

What follows is the migration and cleaning of data, which would usually be scheduled after that, followed by training, and then going live. Timelines for implementation vary from organization to organization, with factors such as the phases (if development or customization is required), to the system chosen by the organization.

Generally, most organizations go from requirements to live in under a year with some doing it as quickly as three months. However, without clear deliverables the project is doomed to failure early on.

3. Customize the CRM System to the Organization

When planning and configuring the organization's CRM system, prioritize the capability to customize it to work for the organization over flashy functions that may not be needed.

This is where the project manager and super users need to ensure that the CRM system fits into the processes of the organization. This means that the fields captured in the data entry interface, the reports, the Key Performance Indicators (KPIs) need to be ironed out and agreed upon by all departments early on.

Doing this when configuring gives the CRM relevance to the organization, as users align the processes they use with what is in the system. In short, it makes sense to the users to include the CRM as part of the processes because it allows them to leverage on the system to share actionable intelligence on the customer.

Ultimately this saves time and grief down the road for salespeople since it is pragmatic and makes sense with regards to current processes, and as a result this benefits the organization's productivity.

4. Test Everything

This needs to be said, but make time to do proper testing and training with all customer facing departments.

The investment in the CRM system is considerable in terms of time, resources, and effort and the impact that the CRM system has on the organization is just as considerable. The project team should rigorously test the system to remove errors, glitches, and processes that do not make sense.

Having these errors in a live CRM system can and will undermine the credibility of the CRM system so ensure that as many issues as possible are removed from the system during testing phase.

5. Migrate the right data

Data migration is the process of transferring data between systems, and can be considered a project on its own.

When switching to a new CRM system, or starting with a new CRM system, data migration ensures that the system comes pre-populated with existing information. It is a huge undertaking and should be given the utmost attention as a technical and business exercise with proper planning and preparation.

As different organizations each have unique business processes and therefore a specific purpose for each of the fields of data, it is important to understand the processes where the data is used and consider the need for each field on a case by case basis. Understanding the old process, and the new (post CRM) process is essential in understanding the need for each field of data. It may be that some fields can be archived, merged with another field, or removed altogether.

Cleaning or sanitizing existing data to remove duplicates, updating information, and ensuring consistency in naming conventions, addresses, and other standards is good practice at this stage. With text memos and file attachments, it may be necessary to file them separately, or store them in a unique field.

Performing data migration with forethought will save users a lot of grief in the future, as data will be better organized and presented in the new system.

6. Launch with a BANG!

When going live with a new CRM system it is important to hype up the launch. Generate interest, activity, and buzz around the new system and the benefits it affords to everyone. A new CRM system needs to be sold to users, and internal marketing should not be ignored.

Internal communication should empower employees, enhance communication between users and management, and give transparency over the project of planning and implementing the CRM.

Some ideas to leverage on this are to write a few articles on the organization's intranet, design a poster, or a commemorative items like coffee mugs and t-shirts. Putting up videos or articles where the project team talks about the CRM philosophy and benefits of the system is helpful in putting a face to the project.

Having an internal launch party with the executive sponsor will also show support for the system and generate activity which will be talked about and remembered.

7. But Introduce Changes Slowly

Habits are best built over time to preventing the user base from being overwhelmed.

With the recent development in user interfaces, most software should be intuitive enough for salespeople to pick up in a matter of days, however using it together with the business (sales) process and getting value from the system may be a bit further down the road.

Teams should start with entering sales contacts into the CRM system, as it gets users to familiarize themselves with the system. Understanding the menus, and knowing the fields that can be found in the system may seem trivial but it builds confidence and activity around the CRM system.

The next step should be tracking individual salesperson performance using the new system. This allows the salespeople to work with their managers on the CRM system, and gets them to use the more intricate functions as part of their daily work processes.

Acclimatizing the salespeople slowly also builds on their foundational knowledge of the CRM using daily routine, and ensures that salespeople do not cherry pick the parts of the system to use.

8. Drive Adoption Rates Up

As mentioned in the introduction, CRM should be more than a technology. CRM should be a philosophy that is embraced by the entire organization.

Implementing a CRM system requires the entire organization to re-think all routines and each individual needs to adapt work patterns to incorporate the CRM as part of their processes. The biggest issue in driving adoption, is that people commonly think of CRM as a tool instead of applying a more comprehensive view of CRM that includes all departments.

CRM Magazine's 2006 issue shows that less than 40% of organizations that implement a CRM system have adoption rates above 90%. While adoption within a department will require time, other departments will have different adoption rates as well, making this is a challenge across all departments of an organizations.

Involving users during the planning and design phases will get buy in from them as they will develop a sense of ownership in the deployment of the system. Gathering feedback is crucial in increasing adoption as it lets users tell the organization what they would like the tool to do, and more importantly how it should be done.

When the CRM system is deployed having patience, conducting training, and corrective behavior will improve adoption rates over time, especially when the steps are taken to ensure that the CRM is implemented and used as part of the organization's processes.

Managing the System

9. Set Up Workflows

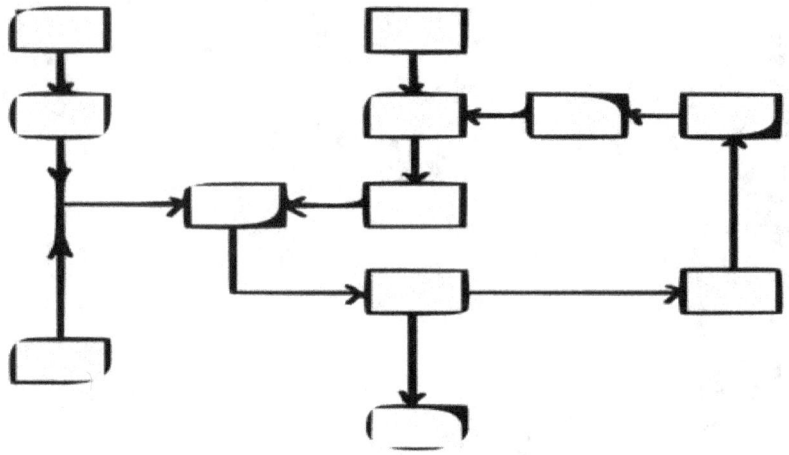

A workflows gives users an outline of a process and a clear direction on what to do during each step of the process; from support messages to feedback and interactions within and outside the organization. A workflow may be a simple list of action items on a "to-do" list, or a fully drawn out flow chart detailing each step of the process it is recommended that these elements are present:

i. Clearly defined stages
ii. Clearly defined actions required at each stage
iii. Clearly defined outcomes required to progress to the next stage
iv. People, tools, and resources that are involved in each stage

Regardless of the number of users in your organization, having a well defined workflow is essential to define each processes. This would ensure the customer experience is smooth when transitioning from phase to phase and a well defined workflow may also transition a customer seamlessly between departments.

Having a workflow also improves training as it ensures that key steps are taken at each stage and allows the organization to scale without compromising the quality of service.

10. Integrate Technologies with CRM

The benefit of CRM systems in these days is that it is constantly improving and evolving.

Application Programming Interface (API) technologies allows organizations to restructure systems to improve collaboration and internal communication. This can result in optimizing and organizing processes, and also provides new and innovative opportunities to reach out to customers and partners.

For example, with many of the CRM systems commercially available on the market there are automation tools such as automated email responders or marketing campaign add on programs.

On the individual level, a CRM system should allow users to schedule, organize, and share clients, prospects, vendors within the organization. Such updates should automatically populate across the system, so information is always updated and accurate. The CRM system should make it easy to organize and categorize leads so interaction with clients can be timely and appropriate.

11. Internal Guidelines

A CRM system is only as effective to the extent that the organization uses it.

If the people in the organization cherry picks the features to use, or if the users are misusing the features, then the CRM will not be able to give its full value to the organization by performing its intended functions properly.

By establishing guidelines and rules relating to the use of the CRM system, everyone in the organization will be aligned with the processes and uses of the CRM system. For example, it should be made a organization-wide protocol to enter every customer engagement into the CRM system. Such protocols will smoothen the transition to, and adoption of, the new CRM system.

It should also be considered that enforcement alone may not be effective and will meet with resistance from users in the organization. Coaching and positive reinforcement may also help in this transition.

At any rate, the guidelines should be written down and made available to all users. It is also a good practice to publish it in the organization's intranet portal, or as a message in the CRM's login page.

12. Encourage Consistent & Regular Data Entry

A CRM system is only as good as the information in it, and very commonly, users will leave out some data from the system due to a variety of reasons.

Training, encouragement, or correction may be necessary to ensure that the data uploaded is relevant and updated. This is especially important in the initial stages of adoption; I have known several sales managers that set aside some time each week for their team to update their CRM and have a super user or trainer available at least during the initial weeks to provide guidance.

Remember that the root cause of cherry picking is usually inertia and unfamiliarity; building good habits with regard to CRM usage will usually overcome most of the issues with data integrity.

13. Use Mobile CRM

Since most CRM systems are now cloud based, that means that they also come with support for mobile devices. Users can access the CRM system remotely, thus increasing their overall productivity. With the pace of business accelerating as it is, being mobile allows salespeople to have access to logs, leads, and customer data at any time. Salesforce.com reported that sales reps increased their productivity by 15% when they were given mobile access to CRM systems.

Being mobile leads to reduced purchase times for the customer, which in turn results in increased profits for the business. Research from Tapp.com has shown that mobile CRM increases the rate at salespeople achieve their targets with 65% of mobile CRM users meeting their quotas as compared to 22% where there was no mobile CRM.

14. Train & Certify Your Users

While there are few people who would argue against the benefits of using a CRM system, but failure to properly educate users on the personal benefits of the system and train them on the proper use of the system will result in a failure of implementing a CRM.

In many cases where employees do not see the personal benefits, adoption rates drop as they revert to old ways of doing things. In cases where there is a lack of training, the system is misused. Therefore, both are equally important when driving adoption otherwise the system will end up being misused or underutilized.

When implementing CRM training, focus on helping users understand the information being presented. Also test the users on what they have learned, and provide periodic retraining and testing to ensure that everything is being retained. Sabre Travel Network, a leading technology provider to the travel and tourism industry, has an internal program to certify each sales staff on different competencies including CRM, and requires a yearly update. These test scores are then shared with sales managers to gauge how well each of their staff are performing in different categories. This could be extended to users from other departments as well.

Also, regardless of whether your organization opts for vendor training or an internal train the trainer system it is important to include an introduction program for new hires. New hires are starting from scratch and they do not have the habits or prejudices that existing employees might have; therefore they may be one of the best advocates for the new CRM system and usually adopt the new CRM system pretty quickly.

15. Collaborate Within the Organization

A well implemented CRM system improves cooperative efforts across departments by making information uniformly available as soon as one party posts an update; as it is said in ManpowerGroup, the third largest staffing firm in the world, the CRM should be a "Single Source of Truth". If a piece of information should be known, it must be on the CRM.

Sales managers often need to know the customer's purchase history, and with CRM it is possible now to have a detailed summary of the customer's purchase history including dates, quantities, and terms of sale. This allows sales and operations to easily follow up when customers want to repeat a previous order. Not having this information easily available will at best prolong the response time, or at worst look bad on the salesperson and the organization.

Customer service representatives are usually the first point of contact for most of the organization's customers, therefore it is crucial that they are trained to resolve customer issues. Customer service representatives should work with the customer to ensure the root cause of the problem is solved, or at the worst case the right actions are entered into the CRM system for a follow up by other departments.

Past issues and their resolutions are equally important to note; most customers want to continue working with an organization they have already have a relationship with and they would want to ensure that past issues have been resolved and will not repeat itself. By collaborating with other departments and being aware of these issues, it allows the department dealing with the customer to be aware of the issues and plan ahead as necessary.

Aligning sales and marketing teams will improve sales by up to 38%. Marketing can see exactly what is going on with the leads they are producing through reporting and ROI of campaigns. As a result the sales department will only receive the most qualified leads based on the screening criteria mutually agreed upon by both departments.

When implemented properly, a CRM system will ensure that when a customer is speaking with anyone from the organization, everyone involved will have access to the same information and customer interaction history. This saves time on both parties explaining the customer's situation and the engagement history to date. Having updated information will ensure that the organization is able to provide the best customer experience, and improve the relationship with the customer. It would seem as though the customer were being handled by a single entity.

16. Automation

CRM systems are designed to streamline processes in business, and one of the ways that it can achieve this is through automation. According to IntroHive, a CRM automation company, the average user spends five and a half hours a week on data entry tasks which may end up incomplete, inaccurate, or being duplicated on the system. They estimate that this costs organizations on average about $13,200 per CRM user per year.

Marketing is an area that would especially benefit from CRM automation. Marketing automation will handle tasks such as batch email marketing, triggered emails, lead management, and campaign management. This allows users to create, manage, and analyze marketing activity with minimal involvement.

Example when a sales representative has contacted a lead and finished with the lead qualification cycle, a marketing automation system can detect that status field and enter that lead in to a re-marketing campaign, rather than leave the lead stale with an unqualified status.

Another area that can hugely benefit from automation is data entry. Many of the tasks can be automated and it is recommended to implement this where possible. This will reduce errors, and maintain the standards of data integrity and consistency. As an added benefit, users will be freed of manually entering the data which allows them to perform tasks with more value and benefit to the organization.

Making use of Data

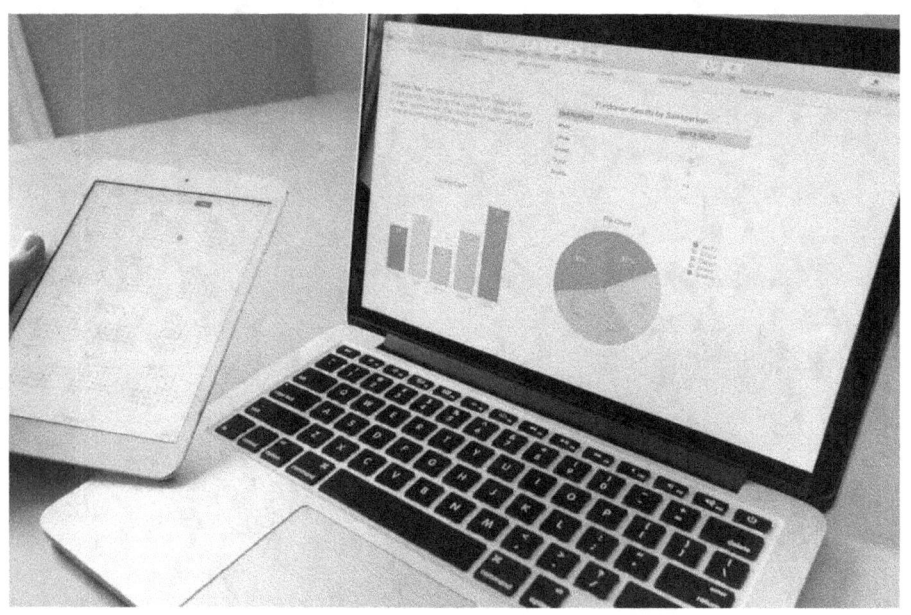

17. Data Security and Compliance

With so much data being stored on the Cloud, data security has become a critical issue; securing organizational data has become a crucial step to ensuring the safeguard of your organization's business, but also your customers' businesses. This is particularly so in industries like finance and healthcare where regulatory safeguards around sensitive data can be time-consuming and costly. A major security lapse or compliance failure can lead to huge financial losses or even bankruptcy.

Rather than constantly adapting to new regulations and reacting to new threats, organizations could adopt a platform that builds those regulations into the process. By embracing a fully hardened CRM system that already guards against these threats will help organizations meet shifting requirements in real-time. Organizations can ensure the security of their data and the integrity of their customer base. While it may be pricey, this is a worthwhile investment in the face of the alternative. As a benchmark, Verizon's Data Breach Investigation Report in 2015 estimated the annual cost of Cyber-crime at US$100 Billion.

Some concrete steps that organizations can take include:

- *Have a defined role hierarchy* - Users are given only as much access on the system as needed to do their jobs.
- *Control access to records or information* - Users can only access the records that are relevant to them to minimize the possibility of data leaks.
- *Have well defined sharing rules* - Define what information can be shared with whom to reduce the exposure of sensitive information.
- *Educate users on security* - Inform users of the value of the data, and the risk that exposure of such data would have on the organization.

18. Defining Metrics and Selecting Reports

Analytics and reporting are key to any business; it is what gives insight into how each department is doing and allows the organization to keep a pulse on things and metrics are only relevant in relation to a strategy or objective, and need to be clearly defined.

In the not so distant past, it was common for departments to have multiple workers whose sole job was to churn out these reports. Now if the organization is using all the features of the CRM as intended, there will be clear, quality, automatic reports being generated regularly. The key is to track the right metrics in order to carve out specific performance and measure it objectively. By minimizing the complexity in the workflow (mentioned above), metrics can be simplified and kept to a minimum. As a result, the number of reports should cover just the processes outlined and a little more if necessary.

Common metrics that are usually tracked are:

- Number of opportunities
- Number of sales calls (sales activity)
- Close rates
- Number of proposals (or bids)

19. Data Policy

Data is one of the most important driving forces of all business processes today, and data policy here covers the general collection, storage, upload, and update of data.

This may seem simple at a glance, but the task is massive. IBM reported that over 900 billion gigabytes of data was generated in 2012 alone and this number grows in each year. It is also important to note that data changes, updates, and becomes irrelevant.

It is important for organizations to have a good data policy as maintaining a set of relevant, up to date, and complete database requires a collective effort from all users, administrators, and executive sponsors. Inaccurate or out of date data will compromise the integrity of the data, resulting in users losing trust in the CRM system.

There are 3 main areas to maintaining a good data policy:

i.   Be consistent with data

Having consistency is important when entering data. By having a uniform standard for how names, addresses, and other information is entered will ensure that reports are more accurate. Search results for one will be hugely improved as results will be more inclusive.

A good practice for data standards is to fully upper case all entries and remove any abbreviations in text fields. Other recommendations by experts include simplifying the data entry process, and automatically populating fields where possible to reduce human error.

ii.   Strive for up to date data

When a CRM system has outdated information such as email addresses, phone numbers, or other information, it means that users will be acting based on outdated information. Emails and updates may not reach their intended recipient, and relationships can grow stale or sales could be lost to competitors.

It is a good practice to regularly verify and update information in the system, usually during or after a sales visit or service call.

iii. Check for complete and correct information

Data often has gaps in fields, or sometimes contain "filler" information where certain fields are mandatory. It is common for users to fill in random, sometimes nonsensical information to move on. This is especially prevalent when the users filling in the forms are not trained, or are from outside the organization.

Without complete information, certain areas of your organization's business process might have difficulty in performing their duties. In such cases, it is common for "data hygiene" exercises to be conducted; normally beginning with an audit to identify the entries which needs to be updated followed by a drive to get users to correct the errors and fill in the blanks. These corrective exercises are tedious and time consuming, especially when errors are left unattended for long periods.

20. Data Mining

The purpose of data mining is to transform data into business intelligence. Data mining is a branch of computer science, and covers the process of extracting patterns from large data sets. This is mainly done by combining methods from statistics and artificial intelligence with database management, usually performed by a specialized department or individual analysts.

As CRMs are designed to capture and organize a huge amount of data, the key to this lies mainly in the organization. Organizations must actively turn the data collected in their CRM systems into actionable intelligence. Some CRM systems come with built in analytics functions, which uses advanced algorithms to mine the data stored within.

Reports generated by the CRM system can be used to produce valuable business insights to make informed decisions. Commonly CRM data is used to improve marketing and sales strategies, or reduce the cost of sales by making processes more efficient. If the organization fails to properly analyze the data that the CRM system produces, then all of that valuable information is doing little more than taking up storage space.

Taking it Further

21. Keeping It Simple

When deciding on which CRM system or upgrades to choose there are many options, and each will be flashier than the last making it very easy to get tempted to buy in to all the bells and whistles. The features available in CRM systems have expanded to extensively cover analytics, campaign management, calendar integration, email marketing, and many others.

However, as adoption increases and your system gains traction, remember that the best features are the ones that are actually needed and used on a regular basis. Salesforce.com found that 43% of users utilized less than half of the functionality in their existing CRM systems. It is not uncommon for some users to look only at certain reports, or use CRM only where required instead of fully embracing the technology.

When considering upgrades it is important to consider the capabilities and drawbacks, as well as to consider its business use. Similar to the planning and implementation process, all upgrades or additional features selected should be simple and pragmatic without compromising on effectiveness. This will help ensure that users take full advantage of the CRM, without getting confused with unnecessary features.

When in doubt, go back to the core principles of CRM; evaluate how these features will ultimately benefit the customer.

22. Personalize the Customer Experience

With the current technology available, more and more organizations are aligning their overall strategy to customer experience. CRM then no longer becomes a record keeping system, but rather one that facilitates communication and processes between departments. Marketing uses it to generate leads, to pass on to sales to generate paying customers, and in turn they pass it to operations and customer service who delivers the product and ensures the customer's satisfaction. In this way, the organization starts to learn about the customer as a whole, and gets a 360 degree view of the customer.

The concept of personalization applies to customer service, sales, and marketing departments equally. All three departments are important to the overall customer experience or customer journey and analytics is the foundation of this. By tracking the customer's preferences, buying patterns, and purchase history, the organization can personalize the service to each customer according to the data collected.

Sending personalized emails based on timely and accurate customer data can increase click through rates by up to 50%. Delivering personalized services or solutions based upon the customer's history with the organization are all possibilities to improve engagement.

Marketing campaigns particularly benefit from this, with 72% using personalization in email campaigns in 2017 according to Forbes. Websites and apps can also be personalized to send marketing messages to match content to their interests or purchase history.

Again, it should be prudent to mention that the process is more important than the technology. Care should be taken to verify the data and personalization to ensure that the interaction is relevant, up to date, and sensible especially in a business to consumer situation.

23. Supplement Your CRM Data With Social Media and Other Data Sources

The customer data in the CRM system is only a partial picture of the leads, opportunities, and customers.
This information can be further enhanced by the use of social media. From Google Alerts for news articles, to Twitter alerts, it is possible to build a better, clearer picture of a customer's organization before engaging them.

A word of caution that with data privacy, looking into personal accounts such as FaceBook, LinkedIn, and other personal profiles of key decision makers or customers might constitute a breech in personal privacy. Looking up the history and social media presence of an organization is generally accepted practice.

For organizations with a B2C customer base, having a FaceBook group (fan page), or LinkedIn group would allow the organization to connect with customers and showcase your products or services. Social media interactions with your users and customers should revolve around education and engagement, instead of just being restricted to selling products or services.

24. Improve Vendor Relationships

The tools and features available in CRM systems makes it a highly effective system for managing vendors and some CRM systems offer add-ons out of the box to manage vendor relationships.

Tracking the relationship with vendors in the CRM extends the value chain in another direction using the same principles and philosophy of CRM. The goal here is to develop a better relationship with vendors by creating a comprehensive view on vendors the same way CRM systems do with customers.

Using these add-ons, it is possible to connect vendors to customer data and involve them with marketing and sales activities, allows the organization to update all vendors about changes in information, or request for quotations using the system.

VendorRisk, a web based vendor relationship management software, simplified the process of vendor relationship management around four steps:

1. Analyzing risk
2. Doing due diligence
3. Documenting issues
4. Monitor the relationship

25. Feedback & Changes

Lastly, remember that the purpose of the CRM system is to benefit the users by enabling their productivity. Changes should be made to keep the CRM system usage pragmatic with regard to the business processes. The effectiveness of day-to-day operations will be your best indicator of whether the CRM is performing its intended task, and if it is not, then how it could be improved.

Very often, where organizations fail is when they try to force a process instead of adapting it to the limitations of their organization. Training, enforcement, and adoption drives may drive the benefits of CRM and its processes. Harvard Business Review in 2004 suggested that CRM projects should be pragmatic, disciplined, and highly focused projects that are relatively narrow in their scope and modest in their goals.

Infrastructural issues that hinder users is especially one area where a pragmatic approach may be needed. For example, hardware issues may lead to poor performance of the system, or legacy systems may not integrate well the new system.

CRM systems have been around for decades, but it is constantly evolving and thus revolutionizing the way that businesses interact with their customers. Unless the organization is willing to integrate the CRM system into its business processes, then it is not going to make much of a difference in the long run.

Conclusion

Thanks again for taking the time to download this book!

You should now have a good understanding of how to get the most out of your CRM. If you enjoyed this book, please take the time to leave me a review on Amazon. I appreciate your honest feedback, and it really helps me to continue producing high quality books.

www.ingramcontent.com/pod-product-compliance
Lightning Source LLC
Chambersburg PA
CBHW030042230526
45472CB00005B/1641